SONGS OF THE NEW DAWN

Selected song-poems of Prabhat Ranjan Sarkar

SONGS OF THE NEW DAWN

Selected song-poems of Prabhat Ranjan Sarkar

Translated by Andy Douglas
Illustrations by Kindle Corwell

Innerworld Publications
San German, Puerto Rico
www.innerworldpublications.com

SONGS OF THE NEW DAWN

iv

INTRODUCTION

Between the years 1982 and 1990, Indian philosopher, activist and spiritual teacher Prabhat Ranjan Sarkar composed over 5000 songs, mostly in the Bengali language. The poems in this book are renderings of some of these songs. Known as *Prabhat Samgiita* or *Songs of the New Dawn*, they were a remarkable achievement, marvels of rhythm, melody, and lyrical inspiration. Sarkar's metaphors for the spiritual life are rich and wide-ranging, his depictions of the natural world beautiful, and his vision of social justice stirring. Most of all, his songs movingly depict the intimate relationship between human lover and Divine beloved. Grounded in the devotional tradition of bhakti yoga, which depicts an embodied Divine, the songs sometimes take the form of conversations, even arguments, between lovers. This relationship consumes the devotee with longing and the realization of the intense love God has for creation.

The best way to experience *Songs of the New Dawn* is to sing or listen to the sung melodies. However, the literary beauty of the lyrics deserves our attention as well. They have been injected with a powerful insight, clarity, sense of purpose, and love-energy. The songs were intended to be used as tools, as devotional and spiritual levers for opening one's heart and expressing the infinite desires within.

Ever since I visited Sarkar in the mid-1980's, I have loved these songs, and felt a desire to help capture in English the magic and mystery, the literary depth and beauty, that the Bengali songs convey. I decided to try to render some translations into a poetic form. A certain amount of license has been taken. You could say that these poems are inspirations, not strict or literal translations. I like to call them 'transpirations.' To transpire is to transform subtly from one state to another, as a plant does with water vapor to air. To transpire also means to 'become known.' The lover wants his/her love for the Beloved to become known, and I would like these poems to help this devotional process become better known as well.

I have studied and can read the Bengali language, but I am not fluent. I'm therefore indebted to the translators who went before me. I was able to look up each word in the Bengali dictionary and ponder appropriate and meaningful possibilities and compare them to extant translations. At times I consulted with native speakers. I strove to find a balance between the original spirit, rhythm and meaning of the lyrics, and a poetic, literary, inspiring sensibility of the word's meanings in English. I also put them into a form which better suited poetic representation, occasionally rearranging line breaks, stanzas and adding enjambments. In order to give the reader a taste of the original language, first lines of each song are printed as song titles, in a Romanized version of the Bengali script, with the appropriate diacritical marks.

I am fortunate to have collaborated with a talented artist, Kindle Corwell, whose scratch drawings remarkably convey subtle aspects of these poems and bring out even more of their beauty.

I consider P R Sarkar not only one of the great minds of the 20th century, but also my personal spiritual guide. My life has been transformed by his teachings. My hope is that readers will be inspired by these song-poems to look further into his work: the songs, certainly, but also his spiritual philosophy, social teachings, and life projects aimed at creating a more just and loving world. For example, Sarkar developed a profoundly ecological philosophy called Neohumanism which calls for extending our love and respect not only to other human beings, but also to plants, animals, and the inanimate world. Hundreds of schools around the planet are using this outlook as a basis for their educational pedagogy. He also developed a new socioeconomic theory, the Progressive Utilization Theory, a rational and inclusive cooperative-based alternative to capitalism and communism. This is having an impact globally as well.

I wouldn't consider it proper to make money off these songs, so all profits from the sale of this book will go to further the promotion of Prabhat Samgiita songs and music through the umbrella organization of RAWA – Renaissance Artists and Writers Association.

The original songs are available for listening in a number of places, such as prabhata-samgiita.net, innersong.com, Songs of New Dawn youtube channel, or the Prabhat Samgiita Player (app). You may also contact me through my website, andydouglas.net, to obtain a copy of Into the Mystic, my recorded CD version of some of these songs with some excellent musicians. Thanks to Carol Tyx for her support and suggestions.

Thanks to the members of my writing group, The Travelers, for their support. I'd also like to acknowledge the advice and encouragement of the late poet Robert Bly, who read some early drafts of some of these translations.

Andy Alok Douglas
May, 2023

DEDICATION

Offered, as all things are, with gratitude and
surrender
To P. R. Sarkar

1040

ÁJ, CÁNDE MEGHE LUKOCURI

Clouds dart across the sky tonight,
Engaged in a rapturous round
Of hide and seek with the moon.

My heart also wants to play,
And rushes toward the firmament.

Moonlight floating on the river
Dispels any hint of darkness
Lingering in my mind.

In the soft glow of the evening lamp,
I wonder, what meaning can be gleaned
From the days that slide by?

The moon calls out to me,
Then glides on, singing its song.

42

TOMARE PEYECHI

At the break of dawn
I feel Your presence:
Birds chirping in the lotus garden.

The morning breeze blows
Splashes of fountain
Onto the tree-lined forest paths.

I sense You in the ups and downs,
The twists and turns of the road.

When I laugh and dance,
Rhythm and melody conjure You,
As do sweet memories.

The song arising from my heart
Reminds me how I've loved You.

You penetrate my dreams, inhabit
Everything I hear and all that I think about.

I sense You at the break of dawn
Amidst the twittering birds
In the lotus garden.

292

KAĽ RATRITE JHAŔA BAYE GECHE

A rainstorm raged last night
Through the garden of *rajanigandha* flowers,
Unnerving me.

Where were You? Nowhere to be seen.
Typical. You are so indifferent to my fears.

The wind unsettled each sensuous flower bud,
Forcing them to drop their petals,
Sweet fragrance dissolving in moonlight.

And still You didn't come.
Absorbed in some divine mood or other,
You forgot all about me.

The rain even destroyed my guitar –
The one that plays in my imagination –
Its rich sound fading away.

You didn't come. Drifting
In an unknown nook of the universe,
Forgetting me.

While the storm continued to rage
In the garden of *rajanigandha* flowers.

24

HATHAT ELE HATHAT GELE

You stole upon us, a complete surprise,
Then darted off just as suddenly.

In the dark night You flashed a smile,
incandescent, and said,
"Sorry, I can't stay. I'm very busy.

Many people want things from me,
And I have to give them all a little something.

From all over they call and I have to be present.
Where will I find the time?

Some, of course, ask for everything.
And some for nothing.

And it's this last group that really wants it all,
As they desire only me.

I have to answer the call of their hearts.
They love me the most."

911

ÁMÁR GRÁME JÁIO RE BANDHU

Friend, meet me in my home village,
The one on the banks of the *Subarnarekha,*
River of the Golden Channel.

A path threads the dunes there
And when the sun rises,
The sea and the sky bloom together in color.

That sight wakes me up
And gives me infinite pleasure.

River hawks circle the far bank there.
In the cashew orchard
Dappled birds dance.

Pushing his boat into the current
A sailor embarks on his long journey from there,
Listening to the song of the river.

Lost in contemplation,
He moves forward, to the sea.

4014

VASANTA ESECHE KISHALAYE SEJE

Spring arrives, brimming with tender leaves,
And the earth goes delirious with color.

The scent of sandalwood hangs in the air,
Dismantling the idleness of winter.

The young buds beam with joy,
Softening my heartache.

Whoever you are, listen:
Today, let's just smile and love each other.

Don't stay inside, come out of your houses!
It's no prison out here, it's an open garden.

Forget your grudges, abandon your spite.
It's a new day; speak with new intention.

384

PA´OA´ NA´PA´OAY SUKHE DUKHE HAY

Sometimes I get what I want,
Sometimes I get what I don't want,
Spinning in a whirlpool of pleasure and pain.

In this meaningless, endless cycle
The days drift by, and the bees buzz,
Ever-hopeful, among the flowers.

Why do You hold back Your grace?
Perhaps You're hiding in the core of my heart,
But I don't look there.

Instead, I race around,
Getting, not getting, a musk deer blindly
Chasing its own fragrance.

I become attached to what's temporary.
A frenzied bee dancing with the magnolia flowers.
Why look for permanence there?

Please, take away my ignorance,
Bring me close, keep me by Your side.

Meanwhile, the bees buzz,
Ever-hopeful, amidst the flowers.

322

TUMI ESE CHILE VARSAR RATE

Picture the scene: A rain-drenched night,
Bamboo thrashing wildly in the wind,
A deafening sound amidst the fragrant blossoms.

In a corner of the house,
The young sisters chat and laugh,
Tying their hair back with sprigs of jasmine.

Out of the deepest darkness
I catch a whiff of your *ketaki* perfume.
And feel a little drunk.

That fragrance penetrates my heart.

5

ELO ANEK JUGER SEI AJANA' PATHIK

After what seemed like ages
The mysterious wayfarer touched down,
Shimmering with graceful vibrato,
And suddenly, life brims with music.

I may have lost everything.
I may be destitute, living in oblivion.

But even within this emptiness,
Rhythm reaches out.

A rhythm that calls me to be fulfilled,
Invokes that which is always beautiful,
Fills my life with song.

246

BHARA' BADALE TUMI ESECHILE

My heart thrills when I remember
That sacred day. Rainclouds pocked the sky,
Dark, but luminescent.

A lot of water under the bridge since then.
How many seasons has the earth spun through?

Everyone comes and everyone goes.
Only You remain, an intoxicating song.

Under the rainclouds that day,
Dark, but luminescent,
I fell for You.

1099

DÚR ÁKÁSHER NIIHÁRIKÁ

Why do You stay so far away,
Like a distant star?

Don't You know that with a single touch
You could have me?

This getting-to-know-you process
Is too drawn-out, too lukewarm.

You forget in whose heart You lit a fire.
I didn't forget.

I sit and wait, cradling my gift.
Laughing. Crying.

You watch everything, silently.

1114

ÁKÁSHER TÁRÁ BOLE EKMÁTRA

From out of the night a star declares,
"You are my only friend."

Whirling earth-dust proclaims,
"I desire You, day and night."

The soft southern breeze stirs, announcing,
"There is no one else,"

And the vast ocean waves call out,
"Always and forever I want only You."

Why should this not be so
When every particle of the universe

Measures out Your love?
Tiny sparkles of light adorning the sky,

Dewdrop tears,
Rain showers of affection.

The fragrant pollen carries Your message
On and on, into infinity.

And every atom of the human mind
Sings of the guest who is to come.

4018

TOMAY AMI KHUNJE GECHI

Year after year,
Age after age,

At the helm of this dilapidated boat,
I scour the planet for You.

Pitching across the ocean of time,
Plying all ports,

Searching for Your beautiful form,
I sail every sea.

You never show Yourself,
Never utter a word.

Still I fervently look for You,
Clinging to the tiller of my boat.

Year after year,
Age after age.

1107

TANDRÁHATA ÁNKHI PALLAVE

Someone's light touch
Stirred my drowsy eyelids.

Somebody kindled a flame
In the neglected altar of my heart.

Until then no light had reached me;
I knew of no practice that could ease my burden.

But suddenly the world lit up,
A glittering, bejeweled lamp.

You could say I was not at high tide in my life;
I had no inspiration to move forward.

Somebody broke my deep sleep,
Persuading me to listen,
Saying, pay attention to the call.

1036

TUMI ELE ÁLO ÁNALE

I was mired in darkness
Until You lifted me
Into the light.

Smiling, You said,
"When you feel afraid,
Don't clench your eyes shut.
Open them and think of me.

A rose without thorns,
High tide without ebb –
This is not the way things work.

Understand?
I am always with you,
In pleasure or in pain,
Loving you.

I am yours,
You are mine.
Let go of your fear."

538

ALO JHARA' KON SUDUR PRABHATE

Do you remember when we first met?
The exact moment, the circumstances, escape me.
I only know it was a morning full of light.

I used to be arrogant.
I'd flaunt my intellect,
Flash my book smarts.

Eventually, life brought me to my knees,
And I was gripped by shame and fear.
But even then I couldn't understand You.

Philosophy didn't help much.
Materialism got us into this mess,
Nearly destroying humanity.

It was only once I learned to surrender
That I beheld You coming toward me.
And You took my hand in Yours.

45

BAKULA GANDHE MADHURANANDE

You surf into my garden on a wave of fragrance,
Trailing scent of *bakula* flower,

Darting in
To the rhythm of a honeybee.

"After every end, a new beginning," You say.
"So nothing ever really ends."

The flow of life is unstoppable.
Even in the desert, it never ceases.

We move along on Your waves,
Flow in Your rhythms.

When You are with us,
All obstacles are overcome,

All gates thrown wide open.

88

HEMANTE SHIRSHIRE HAOATE

On a cool autumn breeze
You are coming,
You are coming.

Jasmine leaves
Litter the garden grounds.
Blossoms of Spanish cherry
Dwindle and drop.

The chrysanthemum stretches,
A rosebud opens.
The ginger flower
Is seized with a lust for life.

Bees, humming with hope, soar skyward.
And the cloudless night smiles with stars,
Keeping a vigil until You come.

409

GAN GEYE JAI TOMARE TUSITE

I sing to please You
And to soothe my scorched heart.

My world has taken a painful hit;
I sing to forget.

The thief of time snatches away everything;
I sing to clean the wound.

For a while I was unperturbed
But now my crown has tumbled off.

So I sing to please You
And to soothe my scorched heart.

2677

MEGHER DESHE HATHAT ESE

From out of the clouds, strange lightning
Split the sky, jolting in me a flash of recognition.

There was no time to get acquainted,
No time for desire to spark.

You left without mentioning Your name;
We didn't have the chance to clasp hands.

Astonished by the suddenness of this encounter,
My mind froze.

Questions would come later, after
The enchanting light had vanished.

Yet a hint of playfulness,
Of Your coming and going, remains with me.

210

DIN GUNE AR KAL GUNE GUNE

I was drifting along, just wasting my days,
When enchantress autumn showed up.

Then, drinking in her beauty,
Delighting in her melodies,

I found myself
Seized by the spirit of the infinite.

I became part of You,
Part of everything.

Bursting with energy,
My heart exploded.

So now I say, Come, friend, let's drink
And dance to this intoxicating rhythm.

1976

MOR GHUM GHORE

You crept into my room while I was fast asleep,
Nudging me awake.

There's so much to do today, You told me.
You can sleep when your work is done.

The day's span is fixed, each instant measured.
Once a moment is gone it will never return.

Time marches on, out of sight,
Following its own course

Like a wheel on a track,
Or a thread through a garland.

So don't forget:
This travelers' inn is meant only for light rest.

29

AMAY CHOTTA EKTI MAN DIYECHO

You have given me a tiny brain,
And yet You expect such great things from me.

Through the openings in the clouds,
You are summoning me from star to star.

So much distracts me:
The smell of the earth, the leaves on the trees,
Sparkling river water, bright sky.

And yet, You go on calling me
From between the rifts
In the clouds.

My friend, I once thought You were right here
Beside me.
How is it that You're calling from so far away?

And if I respond,
Does that mean I'll be able to see You again?

89

KICHU PHUL CAY HAT BARHATE

Winter's spell is not quite cast;
A few leaves cling to the trees. Autumn
Will last a little longer.

Hoping to ward off cooler weather,
The flowers stretch their arms.

As for me, I sit and sing, hoping
To feel You near me.

It's true the wintry mists
Don't yet float before my vision,

But it's also true that in the lotus grove
No laughter rings out.
In this sobering atmosphere I have to ask,

Why are You always leaving?

1001

TOMÁR KATHÁ ANEK SHUNECHI

I heard all the stories about You.
But I couldn't wrap my mind
Around the fundamental mystery.

As I cast about for understanding
There arose a dazzling realization:

Without grace,
No one can know You.

How can a raindrop fathom the ocean?
It can't; it simply dissolves.

Trying to assimilate moonbeams,
The lamp loses itself in the moon.

Throughout time You and I have loved each other,
Though I didn't always grasp this.

Arouse that love!
Make our unknown love
Known forever.

1011

SHIITER KUYÁSHE KÁTIYÁ GIYÁCHE

The morning star blooms against the horizon,
Winter fog rising on a southern breeze.

Young leaves awaken,
Nectar streaming from ripe buds.
Blossoms dot the branches,
And the birds murmur and coo.

A warm wave rolls in from the sea and,
Longing for You, I light the lamps.
Suddenly, You're there. A fountain of color.
I adore Your beckoning eyes, Your sublime stance.

Welcome, beautiful one.
Come into my open heart.

1080

ÁLOKER EI JÁTRÁ PATHE

Streams of light flood the path;
Why sit here in darkness?

Whole luminous worlds beckon;
Why do you still cling to your prejudices?

At the edge of the earth,
The borderland is waving you in
With sweet intimations.

It's time to respond.
Stride forward,
This is no time to sleep.

When it comes to you and the constellations,
You're all related.

You're not alone,
Don't be so aloof.
Recognize the connection.

2788

GAN GEYE TUMI PATH CALE CHILE

I remember the day You bounded down the path
And asked me to harmonize with You.

I was standing shyly off to the side, looking on;
I just couldn't come any closer.

Fear and shame held me back.
I doubted whether You were really mine.

Today, poof, all suspicion has vanished.
I'm determined to go

And mount an expedition for You on that path.
I'll search the thick forests and snowy mountains.

If I don't find You there,
I'll search for You in my heart.

1081

JYOTSNÁ NISHIITHE

One night the moon was out carousing
With the dark clouds.

You approached, silently and alone,
And flashed a captivating smile.

That smile unleashed a rain of nectar
That spread over every inch of existence.

Flower petals dropped
Freely from the sky.

Beautiful, charming, forgiving,
You floated down

Into the garden of my heart,
Lighting signal flares.

1101

ASHOKE PALÁSHE DURVÁ GHÁSE

On the shining leaves of the sacred *ashok* tree,
In the flame-of-the-forest flower,

In the verdant waves of fresh grass,
Your beauty shimmers.

The cooing of doves in the lonely forest,
And the rippling stream's murmur,

In the dazzling blue of distant sky,
The dawn with its sweet dance of colors,
The toss of waves on the ocean's shore,
You are there.

And yet, can anyone fathom You?
You are endless.
Immeasurable.

Beyond word or thought,
We glimpse You only by grace.

2746

JEGE A'CHI JEGE A'CHI

The days blister with heat.
The nights drown in darkness.
I stay up late waiting for You.

Look, I know I'm not alone,
But it's so hard to find You,
And sometimes I turn frantic.

Confronting the vastness,
What can I do but sing
Until I lose track of myself?

Still, I'm ever hopeful;
I think about You often.

Like the mythical *cakor* bird
Soaring across the sky
Ever in search of perfection.

130

SONALI BHOR JIIVANE MOR

Could it be
That my best days are returning,
All the dark pain and humiliation
Gone?

How many potent evenings,
Magical mornings,
How many cool spring days
And warm autumn nights
Did I waste?

And how many hopes drifted away
On a cascade of tears?

But now, as the tender dawn smiles
And the fragrance of flowers hangs in the air,
The memory of pain is washed away.

A new joy for a new year.
Could my best days be returning?

7

NIIRAVATA' MAJHE KE GO TUMI ELE

Who are You?
Breaking the silence, rousing me from sleep.
Who are You?

The storm may rage,
Fierce winds blow out my lamp, but You kindle
The light of understanding in my eyes.

This world is a treehouse in a rain-soaked garden
Where travelers shelter, forgetting for a moment
They're on a journey to some far-off place.

They remember their destination
Only when the light from Your beacon
Strobes across the path.

199

HIYA'R MAJHA'RE NIIRAVA PRAHAR

In hours of quiet solitude
I sat, my heart quivering.

Someone called to me
In song-language:

"Come,
Now is not the time to be aloof.
Sit next to me."
And I did.

Then, time's surge swept the days away.
Crimson dawns, radiant evenings
Faded into obscurity.

And now I wonder where You are.
Why don't You come?
You don't answer my calls?
You don't respond to one who longs for You?

Even from so far away,
You radiate Your spell.
Your garland binds me.
I don't know what to do.

Maybe garland You back?

1503

NIJERE CHARAYE DIYECHO TUMI

At daybreak You reached out and colored the sun's rays
As if each was a hope-laden dream.

In the garden You generated
A cascade of flowers and fruit, fruit and flowers.

He who had nothing,
You placed in the highest seat.

She who had been ignored
You now recognized.

You provided it all – insight, knowledge,
A song to carry us beyond time and the world.

You gave so much.
But You hid Yourself away.

375

RAUNGIN MEGHE HAT CHANI DEY

On a day like today –
Pink and white clouds beguiling –
How can I stay in my room?

The peacock
Spreads his tailfeathers
And dances into the blue.

I want to sing, and break things,
To erase borders. I want to rush toward
The infinite, throwing aside barriers!

You call to me, always to me,
From between the rifts in those colorful clouds,
And it's almost unbearable…

I can't resist!

12

NAYANE MAMATA'BHARA'

When the mysterious traveler finally arrived,
My heart was shaking with longing.

In His eyes affection shimmers.
A pearl-like smile brightly glimmers.

It's all I can do to keep from staring,
But shyness holds me back.

I wonder, who set these waves in motion?
And where was this bliss hidden before?

1

BANDHU HE NIYE CALO

Dearest friend,
Show me the way, lead me
To Your fountain of light.

I can't bear this burden of darkness
Colonizing my heart any more.

Guide me, wake me, rouse me
From stupefying sleep

With Your songs.
Dearest friend.

281

VISHVATIITA VISHVAGA TUMI

They say You are beyond the world
And, at the same time, within it.
If that's true, why keep searching?

Earth, water, fire and air
Each experience the divine touch.

All inspiration, all beauty, begin with You.
Really, it's overwhelming, this grace.

When I sink into contemplation,
You are there in the deepest parts of my mind.
So why do I keep searching?

550

PATH BHULE JABE CALIA'ESECHO

If You should lose Your way
While passing through my neighborhood,
Please, open the door to my home, come in,
And rest a while.

If You ever happen to look my way,
I beg You, do so kindly.

Time passes, life slips away.
The tide rushes into the sea of forms.
Your silence worries me.

But the flower of hope never withers.
I wait for You with folded hands.

And one day my garland has new buds!
Beloved, I know Your touch
Will turn these buds to fruit.

529

MANER DUARE ARGAL DIYE

I had bolted the door of my mind
And slept in, ignoring the rays of the morning sun
Playing at the window.

My mind was fogged
With unimportant things,
Like space and time.

The way I related to people was based on
The differences I sensed between us.

Alienated, self-preoccupied,
I couldn't see clearly, couldn't deliberate.
I was drunk on materialism.

Forgetting the tranquil waters of pure thought,
My mind was not at peace.

I had bolted the door,
A pillow over my head,
And slept in.

2660

TOMAR DVARE PRARTHANA KARE

When I knock at the door,
Begging for my daily dispensation,
Deep down I know I'm only fooling myself.

Give me whatever You like.
This world is Your projection anyway.
You mete Yourself out equally to everyone,
Yet we all claim You as ours alone.

In good times and bad,
Heedlessly or humbly,
People make their requests.

I don't know what to ask for,
Or how much I need.
My brain is tiny.
I leave it up to You.

1078

TOMÁRE PRIITI TOMÁRE GIITI

They say the mere sound of Your name
Dispels storm clouds.
And the trill of Your love song
Can dissipate the mind's darkness.

Whatever the case may be, mostly I remain
Oblivious of You. I call only when I need saving.

And yet my words, my pain
Always seem to move You.

I blunder along, making a hash of things,
And then I say, "Forgive me."

The persistence of my errors,
My begging for forgiveness,
These things somehow
Manage to stir Your heart.

513

PA'HARE AJ RAUNGER MELA'

Welcome to the celebration of colors!
High on this mountaintop meadow
We swing and we sway, gathering flowers.

Then over the cotton fields we go,
Through the stony pastures,
Not even bothering to stop at the river landing.

The flowers braided into our hair
Flutter in the breeze. We are pulled forward
By what thrills us with its goodness.

Our movement has no end, our dancing
Is life itself. Swinging and singing,
We race ahead, full of joy.

When we don't find flowers on the path,
We become uneasy, and that is why,
Wherever we go, we carry them with us.

241

TUMI AMAR KATA APAN AGE BUJHINI

You were so much a part of me
That I took You for granted, so close
I could have simply called out.

In every tune I hummed
Or rhythm I swayed to, You were there.
The sound of Your guitar still rings,
Though I never paid attention to it.

I passed through some dark periods
And would think about You from time to time.
But why didn't I hold You tight?

Why wasn't I able to keep You close?
Perhaps my callowness offended You
And You went into hiding.

1037

KÁCHE ESE DÚRE SARE GELE KENO

Oh, Your hardheartedness is devastating:
You drift tantalizingly close,
Then flee the scene.

You deposit me on the top branch of the tree,
Then yank away the ladder.

When I reach hungrily for the custard apple
Dangling in front of me,
You casually toss it into the river.

In spring You awaken the tender buds,
Only to scorch them to ashes
With summer's searing heat.

You light the lamp,
You blow it out.

All this is squeezing the juice from my green heart.
Is it too much to ask
For a speck of grace?

Something to keep me going
Until I can become one with You?

1003

TUMI ESECHI BHÁLOBESE CHILE

You came, You loved, and You left.
Can You explain this strange behavior?
All this coming and going only confuses me.

Perhaps it would've been better
If You hadn't come at all.

You did leave behind a garland,
Its fragrance intoxicating.

But now the flowers have dropped off
And only the thread remains.
And, oh yes, the memory.

Beloved, our exchange transcended
Pleasure and pain.

When I think about where You were sitting
Tucked inside my heart,
I can only sigh.

183

GA'NER JAGAT KA'CHE PEYECHI

Now that the world of songs is close
I abandon my old ways,

And put aside childish things,
Because when I get You, I get it all.

When a moth rushes the flame,
It doesn't realize how close it is to death.

Sinking into the material world, neglecting spirit,
Is like that.

So I put aside my old ways and run to You,
Captivated by Your world of songs.

Behind all my flitting, my coming and going,
My getting and spending.

You are the end of the story, the final lyric,
The last word.

I forget my old ways
Now that the world of songs is close.

1116

ÁKÁSHE ÁJ TÁRÁR MÁLÁ

The night may be wreathed with stars
But in the absence of the moon
My mind remains dark.

Who carved this ocean-sized hole in my heart?

The garden is bereft of fragrance.
Ice isn't cold anymore.
What's the point of honey?

The peacock's tail feathers are falling out!
He weeps, he mopes, his vitality ebbs away.

The only sound: the restless shuffling footsteps
Of lovers who have lost the beat.

99

BHAVI NIKO ASABE TUMI SHIITER RATE

I didn't think You would come
On such a rainy, wintry night.

After all, this is no night to be outside,
What with the piercing wind
And the doors latched up tight.

I didn't open up and say, "Come inside."
I certainly didn't tell You to come so close.

You came even closer.

I didn't invite You to speak,
Didn't realize Your feelings were wounded.

You gazed into my face,
Then left, following a lonely path,
Heedless of the biting cold.

Not even once did I extend an invitation
On this rainy, wintry night.

94

SHIITER KAMPUNI NIYE ELE

Someone swoops in
On the coattails of trembling winter.

Who are You?
And what's the meaning

Of this terrible beauty
Lacing the fields with ice and snow?

The north wind
Inscribes a cryptic message
On leafless trees lining the lane.

This snowstorm, dispatching shivers,
Seems cruel, a deprivation.

The green world has lost its vitality,
And begins to keen an unknown song.

In the midst of love, heartlessness.
Is this Your beauty?

77

SVAPANE TARE CINECHI

I met You in a dream one moonlit night.
I met You. I met You.

In this dream I floated along a lamp-lit path,
Drifting on a current of melody.

Sometimes the flow of life
Bursts its banks, flooding the world.
When You smile, it's as bright as the sun.

I dance, I sing, the mandolin rings out,
Perfume hangs on the breeze.

Your touch renews me,
And I feel drunk on new light.

I met You in a dream.
And I have You, I have You.

3993

ALOR SAGAR PERIYE DEKHI

Sailing the ocean of light,
I encountered a world on the far shore.
Another world, holding even more light.

In this place
No one languishes,
Everyone flourishes.

The vine-covered trees,
Luscious fruits and flowers,
All dance on sandalwood-scented breeze.

People there speak sweetly,
Offering to listen –
'What can I do to help?'

Water is pure,
Air free of poison.
Produce on the vine has no artificial residue.

There the human mind pivots toward positivity.
No one stews in agony or regret,
And women are respected as equals.

I saw all this,
Crossing the ocean of light,
In a world of even more light.

1106

PRAJÁPATI PÁKHANÁ MELE

Butterfly stretched his wings,
Flitted in, and plundered
Pollen from his favorite flower.

Who knows where he came from?
Or where he later disappeared to?

I wonder if he grasped the essential loneliness
Quivering in the flower's breast?

Weaving together threads of pollen,
He etched a divine keepsake onto the flowerbed.

The flower smiled and said,
Come back anytime, lover.
My heart dances to your song.

1056

TOMÁRE CINEO CENÁ DÁY

I've seen You,
But have I really *seen* You?

I think I know who You are,
Straining my brain
To understand.

Then You give me a loving slap,
Setting me straight,
And I realize how little I know.

When I seem to have achieved big things –
Knowledge, wealth –
I get a little proud.

Then You show me what's really valuable,
And I recognize my poverty.

198

A'MA'R E MANOVIINA' CHANDA HIINA'

My instrument drifts painfully out of tune.
Only Your fingers can coax sweet music from it.

Tell me, if I merge my song in harmony with Yours,
Will I ever be able to play like You?

Whatever I say, You simply sit there, all smiles,
Refusing to come and be with me.

The joy I was feeling drifts away
To some misty land.

Wait a minute. You're looking my way now,
Looking into my eyes!

Yet I can't seem to hold onto You.
Following some elusive melody,
You dance away again.

351

KENO GO E BHAVE ELE

At midnight I called to You
Over and over
Until I got tired
And drifted off.

Suddenly You appeared
In a dream,
And, just like that,
Went away again.

What's going on?
If You come again,
I'm going to hold You
And never let You go.

3992

HE VIRATA PURUSA TOMAKE

Beloved, in the attempt to come close to You
My glorious skill set does me no good.

I give up. My brain admits defeat.
Only love is of any use.

After all, it seems that everyone runs after You:
Sweet innocents, the downhearted and distressed.

This whole earth is nourished by Your love.
If anyone calls it bitter then they don't understand.

You have Your own way of doing things,
And You're not easily moved.

Sometimes You even come with fist raised,
Bent on scattering exploiters and money hoarders.

But in the end, love is the only way out.

329

AJI KE D'AKALE MORE

Today I feel jumpy, alone in my room,
Pushing against my own mind.
A mysterious song rings out.
Could it be You calling?

At the sound of music, the petals in the garden
Open and sway without a care in the world.
Black bees buzz by,
Whispering Your sacred message.

Sunflowers rise to attention,
Shephali trees bow down,
The path is decorated with a mosaic of flowers,
While robins twitter Your tune.

The whole world lies before me,
Enchanted. The music that vibrates
The cosmos
Peals through it all.

1087

TOMÁR VEDIIR TALE BASE

In the dark days of the new moon
I entered Your room, sat before Your bed,
And lit the lamp. The pale light
Was like the glow of a firefly.
Have You forgotten?
You looked up exactly once;
A glance that pierced my soul.

That was then.

Now You seem so far away
And I have lost heart.
Won't You lift me up,
Into the light of truth?
I won't fear the darkness
If You'll keep me close.

337

ALOKER PATH CHAŔIBO NA' AMI

I resolve to speak the truth,
Think noble thoughts,
Live humbly,
And never leave the path of light.

My body and soul will act as one,
I'll do the conscientious thing,
Not yield to temptation,
And walk the straight road.

I've come here to do Your work.
This is the message coursing through my breath.
Awake, asleep or dreaming –
I'll think of nothing but You.

341

DAYAL PRABHU BOLO GO TOMAY

They call You the merciful one.
Seriously?

One who created roses,
But then added thorns?

Who allowed bright alluring streams to burble
Over stones that cut my feet?

And tell me, why does the sweet-smelling lotus
Bloom in such a murky pool?

Are You merciful?

When the stirring starlit sky must fade
Each time the full moon announces itself?

When Earth, our happy home,
Traces such a lonely path through silent space?

When balmy sky and gentle breeze
Turn cruel, unleashing torrents of hail
Amidst the storm's raucous laughter?

And every day, fresh-faced children,
Beautiful as flower buds, fall sick,
Crying long and loud in their pain.

Are You merciful?

101

SHITER SHESETE NAVA PATA'A'SE

Winter's tenure is drawing to an end,
Old leaves dropping,
New leaves unfurling.

Spring raps at the door,
Her braids loosened,
Wild hair framing her shoulders.

Surely the snow will melt soon.
Clinging to this hope,
Wee sprouts peep through the topsoil.

And now, the bare trees burst into bloom.
Clad in new feathery outfits,
The nesting birds recreate Your songs.

Spring is knocking at the door.

112

IISHAN KON'ETE MEGH JAMIA'CHE

Clouds hulk in the east,
And fierce winds squall.

Let's latch the windows.
Hunker down and shelter
From the driving rain!

Outside, precious trees are toppling, fruits
Falling unripe. Birds
Fret and weep over their lost homes.

Fear grips the sailors at sea,
Their ships tossed perilously
On the crests of waves.

Amidst the frenzied ocean thunder,
Spirit dances wildly!

136

AJKER EI SHISHU TARU

The young plants of today
Will one day blanket the desert
With their fruits, flowers, and green leaves.

The call of love demands that we preserve them.
We'll protect you from storm and fire,
Drought and disease.
We're here for you, little trees.

I want to see the arid earth rise
In deep green freshness,
The thirst of the wilderness quenched.
I want to see every desert lush with beauty.

335

TUMI, KON DESHETE JAO RE BANDHU

Drifting on the tidal current
My mind is a dinghy buffeted by the breeze.

We have cut ourselves loose from the moorings
And surge toward the sea.

A mysterious song rings out in the night,
Enchanting us, carrying us far from shore.

Captain, a passionate storm is upon us!
What melody has the power to stir things up
Like this?

Tempest winds snuff out our candle.
My friend, imagine what strange world lies ahead.

3

ANDHARA SHESE ALOR DESHE

SONG OF NEOHUMANISM

I stand in a land of light and lift my voice,
Bringing good news, sister:
A red dawn beckons
At the end of the dark night.

The firmament here is studded with stars,
Air scented with heady fragrance.
You might get drunk on all the pollen
Flying off the flowers, and feel one with all.

The soil where I walk is vibrant,
The land green, and all creatures are loved.
Where I stand the earth dances,
Blessed with life.

1486

E KII MADHURATA´ PAVANE

Can you taste the sweetness
Lingering on the breeze?

Hear the birds
Whistling so melodiously?

Can you say why my mind
Is so full of bliss?

And tell me, what is this love
Filling in the cracks of the world?

Brush the earth and colors,
Shapes and songs stream forth.

Your sweet perfume
Scatters through it all.

I want to watch as You dance,
Feel Your singular rhythm,

And thrill to the trill of Your flute.
Won't You reveal Yourself, please, in these songs?

185

DINER ALOY GANER TARII

When daylight broke I pushed my raft of songs
Into the universal slipstream.

Out of the dancing waves a rhythm arose,
Caressing my consciousness.

I was remembering how You fulfilled my desire,
Spending the night with me.

This morning I glimpsed footprints in the sand
And knew that You were called to leave.

So as daylight broke, I mustered my strength
And sailed my flower-scented scull

Along the song drifting down
From the stars.

168

AJ, ARUN'E RA'UNGA'NO SAB A'SHA'

Today all love is fruitful.
The vine climbing the garden wall
Explodes into perennials
Just as the vine entwining my mind
Bursts with bliss.

Forget the past.
Stroll with me on the beach
Near the ocean of light.
We'll sing of rapture,
How everything is a dividend of love.

Allow yourself to be reeled in by joy,
And we'll merge in each glorious song.

115

VARSA'R RATE TUMI ESE
CHILE RAJANI GANDHA'VANE

One rain-drenched night You floated down
Into the garden of fragrant *rajanigandha* flowers.

Huddled in a corner,
Nursing wounded feelings,
I locked myself in the house
As You wandered the grounds.

The storm raged on, pounding the earth.
Awake all night,
You orchestrated the symphony.

Rain poured torrentially,
But You remained alert, roused
By so much love in the garden.

Unmindful, I was closed off in my room,
And only the *rajanigandha* flowers
Knew You were there.

1502

AJANA' PATHIK AJ KENO ESECHE

What mission is the mysterious traveler on today?
Don't you know? He's come to drench
The flowers with nectar.

Clutching His cosmic paintbrush,
He dyes each petal lovingly by hand.

Open-faced, tender-hearted,
He skips through the garden.

Life's rhythm flows through Him,
A gift of love.

Straightforward, simple, smiling.
No one is strange to Him.

He is...
Beloved.

316

TUMI ELE CARI DIK
RAUNGE BHARE UTHALO

At Your gentle touch
The smiling sun shares its sweetness,
The world flares into color,
And earth surrenders its suffering.

In this joyful atmosphere,
People hug one another,
Leaving sorrow in the background
And stepping up to a vibrant song.

Grinning oarsmen ply life's boat
Toward a golden shore. One flash of light
And we all become drunk,
Dancing in ecstatic rhythm.

306

SUNDAR MADHUR PRABHATE

On this gorgeous morning
Someone special has arrived
Trailing clouds of sweet fragrance.

Reaching out, You brushed the stem
Of a garden plant,
And a cascade of buds drizzled down.

Seeing this expression of joy
The entire garden began dancing madly.

Who are You?

I remember now!
You left one rain-soaked night, Beloved.

The look of affection You gave me then
Turned my heart inside out.

342

SUMUKHER PANE CALE JABO AMI

With Your name on my lips
I'll move forward,

Feet placed firmly,
My heart unobstructed by fear.

Neither mountains nor oceans
Can get in my way.

I'll do the work I came to do,
Confidently, unwaveringly.

I won't grieve for days passed.
And I'll have no doubts about my future.

72

MAOMA'CHI GUNGUNIYE

Sitting here in this garden, I soak up
The bold colors, the musky fragrance of the earth.

Suddenly, drifting in from the vast desert,
A mysterious rhythm envelops me.

I decide to fashion a gift for You, a garland,
Full of whatever sweet associations I can muster:

The nectar buried in the flower bud,
The fragrance hidden in the pollen.

The buzzing of the bees,
The love deep in my heart.

This mysterious music awakens it all,
More sonorous than a guitar.

I sit in the garden
And the bees whisper all around me.

5018

AMRA´ GAŔE NOBO GURUKU

Let's build a new school,
Forge a new pedagogy.

One that wreathes everyone together
With bands of love.

Each flower bud will be tinged
With the light of wisdom,

Each string strummed.
In this family,

Not a soul will be left behind,
No one bereft or destitute.

What an incomparable joy:
All hearts dancing as one.

3995

JAY GAI JAY GAI MANAVER JAY GAI

We sing a song of victory,
The formation of a true human society.

In our hearts, one person is as good as another,
One country as beautiful as the next.

The same sunlight warms each back,
Same vital energy percolates in each bloodstream.

All run after the light of hope, and everyone,
Given the chance, will lift a child onto their lap.

All are ready to receive,
To drink in what wise ones have to offer.

High or low makes no difference.
We're all sisters and brothers.

4761

TUMI AMAR DHYAN, TUMI AMAR JINAN

Fount of meditation,
Source of knowledge.
You are my whole world.

When You're not around,
Longing consumes me.

When You re-enter my house,
I laugh like a madman.

You are the essence of life,
My everything.

Your crimson glow etches the horizon.
Your golden light

Radiates across the firmament.
And under the sweltering midday sun
I sense Your intensity.

I know You were watching out for me
At the dawn of life,

Serving as inspiration for my actions
In adulthood.

Now, as twilight closes in
I'm ready for You to reveal Your final mystery.

1104

KENDE KENDE KATA KABARI BANDHA

My friend slumps in a chair,
Weeping, disheveled, unable to sing.
Who is worth all this misery?

Daylight fades, evening coming on.
My friend remains in her garden,
Crushed, overcome.

Listen, friend, even the swan,
Though he flies far away,
Returns, eventually, to his nest.

If your lover has gone off somewhere,
Won't he return again, too?

563

ALOR DHARAY TUMI BHASO

We might be oblivious,
But You're always there,

A light floating in the darkness,
A constant love.

Your existence stretches back in time
And far into the future.

Even if no one shows up to do the work,
You turn out for us.

At the end of the day
When evening falls

And all my friends have headed for home,
Only You remain with me.

Even if no one listens to Your call,
You still speak so sweetly.

461

TUMI KAHAR TARE ACHO BASE

Tell me, why do you sit
Alone on this shore?

It's my job to convey the boat of forms
Across the ocean of formlessness.

Rowing against the stream of time,
Which has no beginning or end,
Forgetting no one, I keep moving.

Neither philosophy nor science
Can explain what I do.
No rationalization will suffice.

It's just that, at the end of the day,
People get tired.
Everyone wants to return home.

The weary traveler stands on the bank
Hoping for a boat to come along.

That's my cue.
I'm always ready,
And I never delay.

391

COKHER JALE BHIJIYA' GIYA'CHE

The sun sinks and evening descends.
Tears soak the garland I created for You.
There's nothing I can say,
So I say nothing.

You promised to come, but instead You left.
So much time has passed, and You, beloved,
Have still not returned.
I'm so sleepy, and night is coming on.
Perhaps You don't understand how painful this is.

I see now that those who come, will always go,
And those who leave, will one day return.
What I long to realize
Is how You are hidden everywhere,
And whatever plea I make, You are bound to hear.

1012

TUMI JÁNO ÁMI JÁNI

Days repeat themselves, frittered away.
The nights only tell tales.

Who can I share my anguish with?
My tamped-down grief
And barely-concealed longings
Burn within.

How many more mirages will vanish
Into thin air? How many hopes
Float away on the wings of deception?

You and I know the answer to this.
We share a secret:
We have someone to call our own.

211

DIN A͞SE A͞R DIN CALE JAY

The days come,
And the days go.
Nobody knows
What's behind it all.

Sometimes I'm conscious,
Other times oblivious.
Like the days I drift,
Half-asleep.

I have so many questions.
Where did I come from?
When? Why?
I forget.

One thing I do know: You are mine,
And You know what I need.

120

SHARAD PRATE MOR EKTARATE

On this brisk autumn morning I take my seat,
Plucking a single string of my guitar,
While the scent of night jasmine lingers in the air.

A soft breeze grazes dew-soaked grass.
The whole world seems to sway in rhythm.
The birds stretch their wings, soaring across the sky.
The clouds, too, chase a path of light.

This morning I feel the kiss of vitality.
My mind grows bigger and floats into the beyond.
All while the fragrance of night jasmine lingers.

When the floodwaters ebb,
Once-submerged lands are revealed,
A world clad in new clothes.

I don't know whether it was from this earth
Or from realms above,
But You came within our grasp.
And the scent of the night jasmine lingers in the air.

919

TOMÁR NÁME GÁNE HOYECHI TANMAYA

Call me a wanderer on the path.
When I move, chanting Your name,
Singing Your song,
My bonds loosen, and I am free.

You sit, silhouetted
Against the red dawn,
A mysterious melody
Echoing across the landscape.

These restless eyes are soothed
By the beauty of Your form.
The lure of the world lessens
As my mind expands across the universe.

Tonight, I'll row my skiff
Along the floodtide of love songs,
And wait for the shimmering moon
To shed its radiance over me.

ABOUT THE TRANSLATOR

Andy Douglas is a writer and musician, and student of P R Sarkar's teachings for forty years. He holds an MFA in Nonfiction Writing from the University of Iowa. His two previous books were "The Curve of the World: Into the Spiritual Heart of Yoga" and "Redemption Songs: A Year in the Life of a Community Prison Choir." He lives in Iowa City, Iowa. He has been working to expand his heart, let go of his ego, and remember the 'honey-knowledge.'

ABOUT THE ILLUSTRATOR

Illustrator Kindle Corwell is profoundly grateful for this opportunity to visually express the exquisite energy of Spirit flowing through these poems, and for this chance to collaborate with her friend and colleague Andy. Kindle makes her home at ElderSpirit, an intentional community in southwest Virginia.

Made in the USA
Monee, IL
16 September 2023

42677323R00073